Published by Nadia

Copyright @ Nadia Violette 2023

I do, though, give you permission to quote this directly with my author name 'Nadia Violette' if you want. That works!

Thank you for buying this poetry book! As I am dyslexic, at times I've purposefully written my poems in ways that don't always follow expectations around spelling, grammar or traditional poetry formats. Here's to disabled pride. Enjoy!

CONTENTS

Autistic Intensity Poem   06
Repetitions Poem   09
Golden Colours Poem   13
Conserve Me Poem   18
The Blues Poem   19
Plumwood Poem   20
The Wisest Rain Poem   21
S.A. Taboo Poem   22
Neuro Diversity Poem   23
Autistic Masking Poem   24
Stretched Poem   25
Grief Poem   26
Feminist Theory Poem   27
Fractured Teens Poem   28
Static Vision Poem   30
Hygge Poem   31
Mirrors Poem   32
Surviving D.A. Poem   33
Alienated Poem   34
Computer Poem   35
Your Fullest Shape Poem   36
Workplace Bullying Poem   37
Gymming Poem   39
You Need Disability Poem   40
Dyslexia Poem   41

CONTENTS

Devil Bless You Poem   43
Vivid Colours Poem   46
Metal Poem   47
Disabled Pride   48
Hyperfocused Poem   49
Positive Negativity Poem   50
Bright Little Boat Poem   53
Eye Contact Poem   55
Non Binary Poem   57
Permanent Change Poem   58
Prominent Leo Poem   60
Steven Universe Poem   61
Consumer Poem   62
Ancestor Gift Poem   65
Video Game Poem   67
A Man's Man Poem   71
Metal Fest Poem   76
Losing My Sh*t Poem   80
Mad Pride Poem   85
Metal Poem (2)   90
Comfy Poem   94
Video Editor Poem   96
Static Vision Poem (2)   97
Love Yourself Today   99

CONTENTS

Nelle Poem   100
Stressed Oppressed Poem   104
They/Them Poem   107
Nature Poem   110
Workplace Bullying Poem (2)   112
Grief Poem (2)   113
Surviving D.A. Poem (2)   114
Directness Poem   115
Chronic Pain Poem   116
Scorpionic Generation Poem   119
Faerytales Poem   124
Loser Poem   121
Beetle Poem   128
About The Author   130

What is my life?   A
Our life? One word   U
Summarised: INTENSE   T
That's me in a nutshell   I
I can't get away from it   S
Believe me, I have tried   T
By this point   I
May as well appreciate it   C
Or get (more) lost
It's the very fabric of my life   I
My existence   N
Let's get nerdy   T
It's actually destined   E
If you look closely   N
At my life's makeup   S
Maybe I'll melt down   I
One day and I'll be...mild   T
But I doubt that somehow   Y
Sometimes. It's like the
Moving pictures   P
Around me are   O
Always bellowing   E
Straight into my senses   M
Right up in my face
My vision becomes a mirage of
Kaleidoscopic lenses and optical
Illusions. Conceptually splitting
The impact of these sharp
Images can hurt
The shouting materiality

Means I can't stop to rest
No stopping to live
Just survive
It's the only sound
The familiar drive
In my life's video game
When I play, the contrast is
Full. The volume is maxed out
Audio clipping, video clippings
Flashing bright red zones
Time loops, it rotates
I can cope because
When everything breaks apart
It disintegrates at the crux
And I finally recognise
The pieces.
Thank the stars!
That kind of chaos
I can work with.
I can manipulate it
Energy enduring
Transfixing
I'm so used to overwhelm
That it makes me steady
The irony is
My extreme reality
Means I can cope

Well with crisis
(Especially
Compared to you)
As it's my normality

That is
Symbiosis
In action

I need you and
You need me

PERSEVERATION

Repetitions. Repeat. Repeated

Actions, topics, behaviours, words

Movements. Clap! Clapping. Rocking

Dancing. Swaying. 'Yays!' 'Wows!'

Body clenching. Tensing. Twisting

Releasing. Relieved

I can't stop myself, really

It's all so involuntary

Hearing, feeling

(Am I imagining?) these

Judgemental norms

Heated frustrations

Steaming. Perspirations

All of these cultural standards

Are taking their toll, on us all

I'm heavily processed and force fed

Each day. There's too many

Lines to follow. Rules to swallow

I feel like I keep making social mistakes

Each moment! It's biting and

Tearing at my memory

Damn! Damning. Even so

I'll give myself a break, shall I?

I'll let myself be a source of discomfort

That's what I feel like I embody

An awkward thorn, stuck, in a body

Sometimes, I don't mind, as I'm deeply

REPETITIONS

POEM

Interested in what this all means
Intellectually. I'll share all this
Because I'm told that
So many people feel the same
We are all the difference
We are all the same
It's simple, it's boring:
All I talk about is paradox
Paradox just happens to be
Applicable to everything. Or so I believe
Intensely. I'm stuck, right there!
Finally comfortable somewhere
I'll let myself listen back
Over and over. Repeat back
Listen! Back and forth
Repeat it back to me
Please. Again and again
Though I have to admit
Even then, I still get annoyed
When I get locked into
Asking the same questions
Asking for the same directions
But I know these
Rhythms are showing me
Something! Important. One day...

'In your own space and time'
I need to climb over

My tight expectations
I'm lucky to be able to
Give myself some
Breathing room
The music and the
Colours
Are all
Detailed
To attention
! The textures
Turn right around
360. The recurring
Beats, tones and
Tempos are being
So kind to me
Dedicated. Bound
Inescapable
Like I'm family.
We are running
At the same pace
Filtered. It's time to
Push through 'cause
We've figured
Our own way out
We've made so
Many improvements
By going over
The same things
R e p e a t e d l y
It's that time again

Time to indulge
In our only occupation
Where's the needed
Recognition? Silence.
I'm analysing
These loops
These flashing signals
And suddenly!
Unfamiliar worlds
Emerge in front of me
Christ! I need to get ready
I need to get steady
Holding on to what I can
My sharp inhales pull this
Moment towards me
I straighten up! I'm all
Contained and abrupt
But pleased I've calculated
These closing results.
We've made so
Many improvements
By going over
The same things repeatedly
It's that time again. Time to
Indulge in our only occupation
Where's the needed recognition?
Wait, wait. Let me take an
Educated guess! It's lost
In all the inequality again

Golden fiery colours   **G**
Have always been my favourite   **O**
When I see them around me   **L**
They break out in bright bursts!   **D**
It's an intense sparkling dance   **E**
Shattering, swirling   **N**
Singing fireworks
I'm spending time   **C**
Being here   **O**
Even if it's only for   **L**
A few milliseconds   **O**
Even if it takes all my   **U**
Concentration   **R**
I can exist in totality   **S**
And the mesmerising
Fire helps me to   **P**
Come back to reality   **O**
Time slows and I can see every detail **E**
The colours twist and cascade   **M**
In a type of beauty I can't ignore.

This September sunlight
Hits me, holds me
In such a different way
An evolving urgency
It's asking for our attention
So thoughtfully that – it's convinced me.
I'm convinced! It's been spelled out
For us so clearly. Just for you and
Just for me! Lucky face

I hear the gentle, nudging reminders
These natural algorithms, notifications
Are flickering and highlighting
The startling life around me
The last sighs of summer
Lightly prod at me. Oi! Oiiieee!
Shimmering. Stinging. Eroding. Erasing
As the subtler beauties are emerging
It's all showing off, really! I love it!
Have you noticed the ways that nature
Demands our total adoration? Our
Encapsulation? Deservedly!
Pining for our presence, devotion
For a renewed religion.
As I'm swimming
I ask for my permissions
Then feel the water
Lilies' leaves carefully
They are invitingly
Laid out before me
The leaf pads feel
Flat and comfy
Against my palms
It's so soothing
Comforting. Bap!
Boop. Boop. Boop!
Secret, dorky high fives
I play the plants delicately
What an isolated sight

What a sensory delight
For my eyes only
I love saying hello to plants
Even if some folk might mock me
That's fine. That's totally and
Socially acceptable
Because they don't see
The same understandings
The same underbellies
That I'm privileged
Enough to see
That's not their fault
Necessarily. Like them
My own actions are
Informed by my own facts
And don't I just LOVE my own facts
My own exacting stats. Memorised
I softly play these instruments
Sounding. Swimming, spinning
Underwater. Overwater. Stopped. Short
As I start to observe my f a v o u r i t e
Visual stims ever! I'm compelled
Over the water's brim and
Watch the surface rippling
Away. These visual melodies
Are imprinted onto my mind
I'm fully absorbed and I can't ignore
These gorgeous repetitions
Repetitions. These paintings
These never ending
Reflections

A natural indoctrination. I'm ortho doxxed
And fulfilling my selfish agendas
How do I describe these things?
God. I really don't know...
It feels impeccable
Impossible. Our language
Our culture is not built for it
Maybe my dyslexia
Will do the trick.
As I walk down
These streets
It starts to rain
And the world seeps out!
Spluttering at the seams
It's all the same
It's oozing out
Everywhere at me
My static vision starts up
Brightening up
I watch the colours'
Translucent stars
Dance up the
Walls of these
Multiple, shifting
Fractal corridors
They fill up and
Transform around me
Is it reassuring
That I'm 100% sober?

Maybe. If I'm honest
It is a thing of beauty
To live a life in synesthesia
To live a life in
This type of vibrancy
In these special moments
I slowly chew and digest
These new surroundings
Pondering, provoking
My love of life
I watch amused
Amazed
As all the metal
And the plastic
And even the cement
Is glistening
From the rain

Draped, dropped
Dipped in a glaze
Emersed, enmeshed
Life is frozen in a daze
Momentarily inhabiting
Wiser, deeper tones

You finally recognise   **C**
Sacredness   **O**
Necessary as it is a   **N**
Conservation category   **S**
C o n s e r v a t i o n   **E**
To prevent our depletion   **R**
                          V

It's time to savour some   **E**
Loving attention   **M**
Time to use   **E**
Our senses
For an older   **P**
Type of empathy   **O**
                          E

Let's reveal   **M**
A type of divinity
Which even
Secular sights
Can see

Lying in blues
Little lines of light
Shards
Cut!
Through
My compartment
My box of existence

My consciousness
Pulled itself
Back into my head

Painful! Flashes!
I was born into rage
I roll over!
Hands over head!

Red waves keep
Hitting my chest
Heart. Throat
I'm sealed shut.

Still grieving. Fine.
Maybe I always will

T
H
E

B
L
U
E
S

P
O
E
M

Cruelty **P**
Drains away **L**
Life force **U**
That's a proven fact **M**
I bet you're not *actually okay* **W**
With doing that **O**
To someone **O**
Am I right? **D**
Anti oppression work
Has so many needs to meet **P**
Let's take some **O**
Sacred responsibility **E**
So we can embody **M**
Equality and love
Exactly like we claim to
Let's do our jobs, our duty
Let's sleep soundly at night

After a day of talking T
About that difficult history H
I was wobbling as a human being E
On various wavelengths
No longer able to compute W
Crossed signals I
They said it seemed like S
Complex PTSD. But who knows? E
Who cares? Human malfunction S
I stopped as we were walking T
Together. Brimmning with
Sadness & frustration & all too R
Familiar forms of suffering A
'I don't work'. I cried. I
Crunching. Blistering N
Collapsing. Breaking
Panicked as life P
Was cutting O
Away at me E
And all I could feel M
Was a desperate need
For it all to stop. Human
Malfunction. Error
Error! Please.
Send me
Some anti
Virus software.
And then I was met
With the warmest of care
Right there. In the wisest
Rain of all

The stigma
Is all that's left
I have gone
Through all the rest
It's been quite a lot

The stigma
Is all that's left
& you are upholding it
As I'm dangling
At an angle
In the air

I should have *never*
Spoken to you again.

The stigma
Is all that's left of me...

S
·
A
·
T
A
B
O
O

P
O
E
M

Many nouns mirror N
Those mental landscapes E
Dissociation U
(Amnesia, depersonalisation R
Derealisation. Identity confusion O
/ Alteration). Gender dysphoria
Anxiety, OCD, autism, ADHD D
Talk about cognitive ambiguity I
What a ridiculous vocabulary V
Kind of. Kind of useful E
Actually! R
At the same time S
I want it all nullified I
As I think that this is T
A type of normality. Y
Complete expressions
Of human diversity P
O
E
M

Expected to shun
My own agency
So brainwashed
I find it almost funny
As I observe myself
Obeying
No longer driving
Dying. I sit, I smile
And feel myself
Surrender
To watching
My own life's
Reality TV
Self-policed
Nails gripping
Into the chair

A
U
T
I
S
T
I
C

M
A
S
K
I
N
G

P
O
E
M

Pondering   **S**
How can I   **T**
Maximise   **R**
My potentials?   **E**
My precious moments?   **T**
As life seems to be   **C**
Speeding up   **H**
S t r e t c h e d   **E**
Unevenly   **D**
Exponentially
Like the Universe   **P**
Like the world's   **O**
Technologies   **E**
Its knowledges   **M**
Everything is
Expanding so rapidly
Uncontrollably

But! Let's take
A moment to
Slow things down
Let's sit back, for now
For a while. Allow
Ourselves to inhale
For real this time

And watch all of
This pronounced
Beauty unfold

A period of loss   G
Of grief. Has forced me   R
Into a new place   I
It brutally shoves things   E
Into their shining   F
Perspective
Teaching us how   P
To be our most effective   O
Timely. To make the most   E
Of our moments   M
Of our relationships
Love is showing me
Its many shades
And in this rotten grey place
The many paths that
Were before me fade away
There's only one left because
Everything is clearer now. Refined
Being overwhelmed by life
Is humanities fate
So is being
Trapped in a body
Temporarily. We are
Still stuck behind these
Soft, strange, physical gates
Thankfully! Once we have opened
And into death we pass
Only love can survive
Its deafening grasp

I can feel the thoughts
Knitting together
Into something else
These are pensive wombs
Birthing evolutions

With these wise words
They pass me the dressing
With which we are addressing
The wounds of the world

F
E
M
I
N
I
S
T

T
H
E
O
R
Y

P
O
E
M

'Thanks' for this   **F**
Unique experience   **R**
Aren't I lucky   **A**
To know this foresight   **C**
Mixed up. Meshed up   **T**
I'm messed   **U**
Tentatively awake   **R**
Like blips of a heart beep **E**
Awake on heart machines **D**
Monitoring our time
'Stop wasting my time!'   **T**
That's what these   **E**
Memories do   **E**
Waste my   **N**
Awareness. They   **S**
Shorten my timespan
My schedule. I'm stuck   **P**
In another time   **O**
Please wake me up   **E**
My brain is lighting up   **M**
Lightening up
You're wasting
My current being
Present time
Precarious. Precious.
Present in being
This being

Thanks at least
For giving me
This body
And mind
To focus
My attention
So when I'm free
As I please
I'll damn well
Enjoy it
To the
Extremes

Synchronised melody
When it moves away from me
I can feel it fracture
Ricochet
Off the walls
Off the furniture
I feel just
Outside of myself
That suits reality
Doesn't it?
As I'm not
'Just' myself. Am I?
Swallowing my moments
& reliving my past

It's too much
For my little frame
My little frame
Of theory that
Compartmentalises
Me. These are
The structures
We cling to
That we must
Morph through

S
T
A
T
I
C

V
I
S
I
O
N

P
O
E
M

Cosy **H**
Warmth. **Y**
Comforting touch **G**
Happy laughter **G**
Tinged with **E**
Sadness
Always **P**
With depth **O**
This familiar **E**
Nourishment... **M**
This love.
It makes a life
That is worth
Living

Mirros   M
Only show me   I
What isn't real   R
Perhaps it will be one day   R
Perhaps I can see my future   O
Aged. 'Disproportionate'   R
'Ugly'. 'Wrong' and in   S
Unfamiliar territory
An imagined   P
Monster is always   O
Staring back at me   E
So vibrantly self critical   M
I partition myself into bitsss
Portioned. Chopping myself up
Into unfair slices and segments

And whilst I know
These standards are made
It has also been how
I have been made

Forever eluded?
I don't even know
If I will ever
Have the ability
To truly see myself

Sometimes
I really don't want
What life has to offer
I can't bear
Its consequences
The ones I didn't make.
I can't bear it here

S
U
R
V
I
V
I
N
G

D
O
M
E
S
T
I
C

A
B
U
S
E

P
O
E
M

I have been   **A**
Far too interested   **L**
In being alien   **I**
                               E
At some points   **N**
All has been   **A**
Otherwordly   **T**
To me   **E**
                               D

But we have
Been gifted   **P**
Physical form   **O**
To manifest   **E**
Physical change   **M**

And *right now*
Is the time
To honour
That fact

Finally I spread out the time
I need to fish through
Hundreds of bright layers

Clicking, ctrling
Through screens
Finding what I need
What I want
Mind wired
Correctly
Temporarily
Forced to function
At maximum capacity
Present intent is
Streaming through
Whilst my hands and
Wrists are aching

Plugged in
Aren't I technology?
Kept back by biology
Humming to
Mind blending tunes
That put me back in my
Rightful place

C
O
M
P
U
T
E
R

P
O
E
M

Sensuality allows me   Y
To exit into the present   O
Into a place of peace   U
A rare insight   R
I'm exhausted from
Destructive scenes   F
                              U
The tipping point for me   L
Is feeling into the now   L
It's time to get out!   E
By noticing the present   S
By noticing your exact placement T
Now. Because most of our pain
Starts from somewhere else   S
In a land far, far away   H
                              A
Flesh our your experience   P
By appreciating   E
The smallest parts
Hear the texture   P
Of the tones   O
The grades of sound   E
                              M
And draw yourself back
Into your fullest shape

Each day is a new day
Of denigrations
Further eroding worth
That's vacant
For what it's worth
Each day, new lies
Defences, reality
Check. Ing

Using my devalued parts
Against me, on the daily
As if I was an easy target.

As if!

I never thought
Adulthood would be
Childhood. Repeatedly
But that's a child's naivety
And I never thought
I'd have to revisit my past
In the immediate
So frequently

I thought I was doing okay
But it seems I have
A lot more to learn
From the hard way
What have I missed?

W
O
R
K
P
L
A
C
E

B
U
L
L
Y
I
N
G

P
O
E
M

What I am
Responsible for?
I know I can survive
But do I even want to?
As this life
Will mostly be
A type of intensity
That I don't feel
Able to endure
I'm endlessly
Over my full
Capacity

Gymming	**G**
Exercising	**Y**
So many	**M**
Mixed feelings	**M**
Spiky sensations	**I**
Rushing around	**N**
Resentment	**G**
Euphoria	
Boredom	**P**
Like I'm totally	**O**
Healthy again	**E**
(Was I ever totally healthy?	**M**
What does that even mean?)	
I start easy	
I'm not at all bothered	
Then when comfortable	
I push. I try harder and	
Enjoy the difference	
The contrast I feel	

NEUROTYPICAL   Y
Bother to listen   O
Make yourself care   U
For once
I've spent   N
My *entire life*   E
Learning, trying   E
To emulate, understand   D
Assimilate. Your world

           D
There are privileges   I
From your insights   S
Life upgrades   A
There are privileges   B
From mine too   I
And you need   L
Both treasures   I
To level up...Look around   T
You should know by now   Y
That you won't get far...
You won't get anywhere   P
Without us   O
           E
           M

The reason I can make my poetry   **D**
Is *because* I'm dyslexic   **Y**
My speciality   **S**
Grammar, spelling   **L**
It won't always be   **E**
Conventionally perfect   **X**
& I think that's a fair trade   **I**
I use different words   **A**
Phrases to what is expected
They play around in my mind   **P**
Making striking movements!   **O**
Conversing, flirting   **E**
Like a dance   **M**
Of meanings
They are
Precisely
My feelings
Me. Lexxic diversity
Is natural within
Without. Strict created
Colonial, classist rules
In this constabulary
Judging people negatively
For writing and
Speaking differently
Isn't that more about you?
I celebrate being
A disabled person
Try it. Really
Bother. You need to

Because it's society
That 'disables' people
The way my words work
Is unique to me. Don't make them
Inaccessible! They are a visual puzzle
I piece together moments
And 'mistakes' that
Seem to make exact
Sense to people
Funny that...
I love my bumps
And unusual
Ways of using
Creating. Distorting
Words. Of thinking

You're theoretically
Uncomfortable?
Good. My job.
Sit in paradox, for once
In 'error'. Because maybe
It's your outdated theory
Your reductive
Oppressive
Overly restrictive
Forms of communication
That don't make sense

A Devil.	**D**
Seen as a	**E**
Daughter	**V**
When I'm not	**I**
Treated like	**L**
I'm *always guilty*	
When, I'm not?	**B**
Guilty for just being here	**L**
Just about! Judging by what I know	**E**
Being likened to a Devil	**S**
As I have been	**S**
It's a good thing	
Theoretically, morally	**Y**
But practically	**O**
It's scary. Ostracisation	**U**
Leads to precarity	
So-called 'madness'	**P**
(another semi-made up story)	**O**
Then further vulnerability	**E**
It's society's spiral. It's	**M**
Standard. Structural	
I have watched	
People demonise me	
In order to hide	
Their own cruelties	
Like I'm Witchcraft	
Or certain	
Class A drugs	
I am after all an	
Easy scapegoat	
Am I not?	

I've fought, naturally
Gave the damaging
Norms some clarity
I'm here to destabilise
Some privilege -
Apparently!
Wasn't my intention

You're welcome

Maybe that IS the Devil's work
That part has been a pleasure
My loved ones. My hated
They'd rather crush me
Conceptually. Than be
Accountable
Obviously

Can't you see?
If I wasn't 'mad'
There'd be something
Seriously wrong with me

What I experience
It is treated like
It isn't real. Like I don't matter
Infinitely inferior. Invalid
They erase each memory

So even if my
Reality did fracture
How would I even
Know the difference?
Think about it. Logically

Just the end results
Of day-to-day treatment
In this life-minimising reality

I'm telling you
What inequality
Does to a person
This is textbook.
Discrimination.

But maybe
You know already.
And I'm just so sorry
About what's
Been done
To our light

I am vulnerability	**V**
Literal and immediate being	**I**
Sure, I'd rather be 'scary'	**V**
Unapproachable	**I**
Sarcastic. Suitably mean. Polished	**D**
Build that wall people seem to have	
But, my protective layer is	**C**
Unfit for purpose	**O**
A gas rather than a solid. Shoot	**L**
The thoughts, willingness, it's there	**O**
But it hasn't materialised	**U**
I've realised that things hit me	**R**
Like many tiny bullets	**S**
I glare at the glass shards	
In slow motions	**P**
I am reborn on repeat	**O**
Feeling fed up	**E**
Of whiplash but	**M**
I've been made to	
Live out loud	
At full volume	
To live out all of	
Life's colours vividly	

Metal makes me happi ^_^   **M**
Listen to the lyrics   **E**
It is calmness at its purest   **T**
And it reassembles my soul   **A**
                                             L

I remember Killswitch Engage
Lulling me to sleep   **P**
My truest tranquillity   **O**
                                             E
Metal programs my physical world   **M**
And when I'm moving, humming, singing
Along the colourful waves, riffs
It is stimming vitality
Life-giving

The particles move
Into pretty, addictive patterns
And I wish I could show you
What I can see. But maybe
You *do* understand
Exactly what I mean
And if not, I hope
Words, imagery and
Second hand emotions
Will suffice for now

If only you knew	**D**
Exactly how some	**I**
Noises feel like	**S**
Someone is actually	**A**
Shaking me	**B**
How frequently	**L**
I'm made to meet	**E**
Common assumptions	**D**
And behaviours	
That can place me	**P**
In immediate	**R**
And long-term danger	**I**
How much labour it takes me	**D**
To pass as neurotypical	**E**
As 'normal' (it's safer)	
If you only knew	**P**
That listening to	**O**
Our disabled insights	**E**
Could change many	**M**
Worlds for the better	
If you really knew. I bet	
You wouldn't waste a moment	
You'd be damn proud of me	

I am committed to systems	**H**
When I'm hyperfocused	**Y**
Each time...	**P**
It's like entering	**E**
A new world	**R**
A simulation	**F**
Of raw information	**O**
I'm unable to hide	**C**
My enthusiasm	**U**
I am made of it	**S**
Flooded & fully absorbed	**E**
Delightful! Hypnotised	**D**
By stark reality	
And unrecognised	**P**
Processes slowly	**O**
Turn into a language	**E**
I know fluently	**M**

Am I even understandable?!
This brand of comprehension
When you're transfixed
On the important parts of the whole
It means I can pinpoint its exact location
It means I can manipulate things
In the good way

Positive and negative   **P**
Go on, tell me the right balance   **O**
What is the correct equation, again?   **S**
I'm being too negative?   **I**
Too enthusiastic?   **T**
At this rate   **I**
Maybe I should   **V**
Just be numb   **E**
Neutralised
Tranquillised   **N**
By my judgemental culture   **E**
If only I could be but instead   **G**
These common judgments   **A**
Ramp up my emotions.   **T**
People have a fixed lens   **I**
Binaried and narrow   **V**
So me being   **I**
Realistic, different   **T**
Factual, it's framed as negative   **Y**
As criminal. Confusing right?
Don't get me started   **P**
Being confused   **O**
Is a social offence as well   **E**
I wish I hadn't been   **M**
Born without a shell

So I could take shelter there and
Never need to tell
What is made out of
Sense in your absolute social mess!
What do these expectations mean
When breaking a social cue was never
Near my intention.
I was being real with you
I'm sorry about that.
I'm so sorry for yet another privileged
Moment wasted. And I feel so bad
For some reason. Okay. Noted.
Next time I'll try not to be truthful
I'll try to not be myself
A bitter taste of
A society
Of false humanity
Why should I have to
Fake anything with my friends?
That's what they are. Right?
Exceptional circumstances:
If you're really depressed
And you need
To force out
Some positivity
That's different
Sure, we can do that too
But let's actively agree to that
I can be a loving
Distraction

Some light entertainment
Letting me know
Your needs would be better
Than taking your
Frustration out on me
That's on you.
That's your
Responsibility

Things seem at a loss   **B**
But take it from   **R**
Someone who is versed   **I**
In being full blown   **G**
Bloomin' lost at sea!   **H**
                                               T

It serves an ironic purpose
So I don't fight against the tide   **L**
Not here. Trust me. Tough periods   **I**
Can help to ensure   **T**
The very radical changes   **T**
We'll have to endure   **L**
Yes, it does suck. + could we   **E**
Do what we need to do
Without this darker   **B**
Sense of urgency?   **O**
Maybe not. And then   **A**
We'd really be f*cked   **T**
Then we'd actually lose
                                               P
Keep going   **O**
This knowing   **E**
Encouragement   **M**
Warms me
Like a life jacket
There exists
Recognition
That we're lost
We're pretty f*cked

But we're together
So. Whatever.
I know we can pull through
Most hardships with
Well earned skills
And these difficulties
Develop, refine and
Inevitably produce
A tireless balance of life
And, well. I already
Have a trusty map
To hell and back
You can use

We're hardy from
Being human
From our
Immortal hope
So at least
Let's go together
On my bright little boat

Issues with   **E**
Eye contact?   **Y**
My whole life   **E**
I forced myself
Into neurotypical   **C**
Vision. Even though **O**
Looking into your eyes **N**
Is costly. It feels like **T**
My eyes are burning **A**
With data. It's your **C**
Head's heart   **T**
It's as if I can see
Everything in your soul **P**
And vice versa   **O**
The good, the bad   **E**
I know. Ew. I'm not willing either **M**
I don't want the invitation
All of this new, blinding information
All of the old, all of the projection
I don't want to share souls
Thanks for asking
I can't get out of this
Invisible look easily
I'm physically trapped
In this gazing intensity
Help!! They see it
As a dramatic lens
And I'm to blame
For daring to see

I can be a great aim
A locked target
I seem to be
A magnet
For greatness
For illness
For headliners
For monsters
For people
Who are easily lost
The Misinterpreted
The Mistreated

Maybe they
Need some signs
Perhaps they
Are looking for clues
Directions, or familiar faces

Quick! Engage me now
Whilst we are still here
And before the
Intensity fades

Non Binary   **N**
I knew it   **O**
In my bones   **N**
Before I found the words
'Woman' in relation to me   **B**
Always made   **I**
My skin crawl   **N**
If you call me a 'she'   **A**
I'll automatically hurt   **R**
Because   **Y**
It's incorrect
Incongruent   **P**
Incompatible   **O**
It reminds me   **E**
That people   **M**
Don't understand
And many never will
And I don't
Have the energy
To educate
Each living soul
I encounter.

My gendered world
Is different in a
Normal magical way
And I absolutely adore being me
I absolutely adore being the real me

Um...well   P

I know the world is effed up   E

But if it makes you feel any better   R

(Maybe not) it has always   M

Been super effed up   A

Or more often than not   N

And the difference is   E

Now we know why and how (a bit)   N

We can see, finally!   T

We can analyse, recognise, reflect.   C

We can be accountable   H

For the 1st time   A

In modern history   N

In this finality exists   G

Possible redemption   E

I mean, hell, perhaps

This is purgatory!   P

We now have   O

The tools, the sight   E

To radically   M

Change the world

For the better

For the people

At the bottom

Let's reinvent it.

Chop chop!

Even though

I'm stuck in a place

I don't recognise

Even though I'm afraid

I am also excited
Because things
Will always change
Always.

That fact is
A relief but mainly
When you're
In a tough place

There will always be
Something new
And I really
Hope it's
Something
Better

My strawberry blond mane
Looks different each morning
A 'lazy', changing statement
Perfect for my
Malleable character

I'm confident in my fallibility
I get cosy and start creating
I practise
Practise, practise
Then I start performing

I reel most
Of my wrath in
So emotional
Wildfires are not
Constantly pouring
Out of me

Fatigued
It's so much effort
But I feed it all to my
Central engine so
It burns as
Recycled energy

That's what I use
To fuel my
Flaming intent
On life's stage

PROMINENT LEO POEM

Steven Universe   **S**
Makes me so happi   **T**
The cartoon   **E**
Has become one   **V**
Of my special interests   **E**
Thinking about it   **N**
Makes me feel peaceful
I'm colourful, humming, full of   **U**
Gratitude and magic views   **N**
It's one of the best   **I**
Things I've ever seen   **V**
And the only cartoon   **E**
I've ever been reflected in   **R**
Queer, gender fluid   **S**
And neurodiverse   **E**
Also! Video games
Aliens, diversity
What more   **P**
Do I want?   **O**
Nothing!   **E**
Steven Universe   **M**
Is King and Queen
But only if he wants to be
He's held my hand through
The darkest times
We've celebrated life together.
He means so much to me

You know   C
I can never tell   O
If someone is   N
'Flirting' with me   S
I'm told it's a common   U
Autistic happening   M
I've never   E
Been able   R
To do it myself
It's been cancelled   P
Out of my manual   O
Not that I'm   E
Sad about that   M
Necessarily
What a relief
What a mess!
This unsavoury
Confusing, paradoxical
Indirect dance is f*cking silly
Honestly. A waste
Of everyone's time
Just say what
You mean! Christ
But not knowing
Has had its issues
It's dangerous stuff
In this sexist
Ableist world

Being misread or
Not being able to see
People's intentions
I've been taught to
Always follow their
Directives and
Preferences
To place my own
Needs and wants last
If anywhere at all

Why? Don't you
Believe me?
Wow. What novelty
Sure. With my gender
And disability I guess
I'm naturally to blame
When I experience
Harmful behaviours
I mean. Let's face it
Why wouldn't I be?!

This is your disbelief
I'm socialised
For consumption
Not for consent or an
Honest conversation

I know, right?
How dare I. How dare
I speak about my life
My experiences

How dare I try to
Raise awareness

How dare I exist
Outside of
The place that has
Been made for me

Outside of
The grave that's
Been dug for me

A lack of intel has
An expensive cost
In a world where
Double standards
Are standard
And lying
Is breathing

We embody Love   **A**
I can see it   **N**
I thought everybody could   **C**
I think everybody can   **E**
Can't you?   **S**
Skipping, lilting   **T**
Trilling along rapid   **O**
Spirals & happy-swirls   **R**
Malleable dreams stream
Through every pore   **G**
Sparking. Sparkling   **I**
Akasha   **F**
     T

After beaming precision
& dancing our purpose   **P**
Into the earth   **O**
I was full and   **E**
Overflowing   **M**
With gratitude
Naturally
Imbued

As I walked
I could feel the internal
Project external
All around me like a shell

You quickly take it in. Out
Breathing. Exhaling
On life's high

We are breathing oxygen
Onto these embers
Licking our
Lacerations
Soothing
Smoothing out
Sore muscles
Singing dissonant
Spirits back
Into their rivers

I do this
For myself
To value what
My ancestors
Do for me

All our imagination   **V**
And much more   **I**
Is out there. In digital   **D**
Fantasy forms   **E**
Meticulously designed   **O**
To align with us. Precise
Computerised lines, made   **G**
According to our data points   **A**
Our aspirations, our conditionings   **M**
These virtual playtimes have   **E**
Been seasoned
By specialists. By code   **P**
By people pressured to produce   **O**
All these pure experiences for us   **E**
Under strict deadlines. Extensions   **M**
Go on! Give me another
Needed identity crisis
I'm plugged into the system
All my splaying senses
That usually mislead
Me into opposing
Contorting directions
They finally stop messing
Around, which is a nice change
And I happily hyperfocus
Into one specific area
Buzzing. I have these
Extra choices and

My daily life evaporates
I'm living in another
Purposeful environment
I'm a new person
A 'hero' this time
Fully programmatic.
I admire these intelligent
Particles. They are just as beautiful as
The ones in real life sometimes
I know I sound like a loser
And, well. I am
We already
Established that
A long time ago now.
Oh yes!
Proud face
Proud facts
It's true, it's epic
They mean so much to me
These eternal forms
Of entertainments
Though, saying that
Will I be 'too old'
To game one day?
Maybe. I doubt it
But whatever the answer is
I'll enjoy it as long as I can
Video games have made
Parts of my life
So amazing

We all deserve play
We do. It's another
Equality question
Equation. It's essential
For us. I wanna play
I wanna actively
M A K E joy
In childhood
Fun happened
On occasion
But I can only remember
A few instances
Maybe there were more
But I can't remember
Because it was all
Drowned and washed away
In the black and the grey
And now that I'm of age
It's my time to have fun
We.all.deserve.to.play
So no matter
What the norms
Have to say
I'm going to love
My 'nerdy', 'dorky'
Video games. Love
This loud, sense-full
Satisfaction

I've been gaming since
I was 7 years old
So, it's part of my DNA
My first home :) <3
I'm so grateful that my
Real life is very pretty
Nowadays. Still
The outside world
Is still painfully stumbling
Around, whacking
Smacking into
Knocking over
All of our valuables >_<
It can be so frustrating!
So embarrassing
Rolls eyes.
And video games
Provide us with a kind break
And most of all they provide
Me with a well overdue
Celebration

Treat me like a man   **A**
Please. By that I mean
Treat me as an equal   **M**
Love me   **A**
Not as an object   **N**
Or only as   **'**
A hated, wanted   **S**
Sexualised symbol
Or like I will always deceive you   **M**
Like I owe you something   **A**
Like I owe you everything   **N**
As a devalued 'woman'
Because, for one. That isn't me   **P**
And for two, that isn't love, is it?   **O**
Not a type worth initiating   **E**
In any case. These given categories   **M**
Have always felt very unfair, cruel
They feel ridiculous, illogical
Really *force yourself* to
Make me someone
You are willing to listen to
Believe. Make me someone
You are willing to learn from
Someone you are willing to teach
Let's admire, respect, adore
Revere, honour
Idolise, recognise

And prioritise each other
Promise me. Let's *actually love*
Each other equally
It will take a
Lot of active work. I know
Believe me. Believe me
(Please believe me)
I know, as I am just as
Sexist as everyone else is
In this homoerotic culture
A lot of the time
Society's true, automated love
Is reserved for men. A given
And I've always been
Soooooo jealous of that
Since I was a child
That's me! :(

Why don't I get
The same treatment?
I want that. I *deserve* that
Like everyone else does
Don't you want that too?
I bet. It's enraging
Revaluing women
And other genders

Means loving us equally
That of course means
Leaving out all of the harmful
Parts of hetero patriarchy
Directed at men
It harms them
So much as well
We all know the
Same system
Damages us all
That our fight
Is the same fight
Don't we? It always has been
(Haven't you been listening?)
It's important to
Ignore the messages
The BS that says otherwise
The patriarchal
System is a central
Reason for all this
Suffering. I was given
A gendered role
That I have *never*
Identified with
And I have been
Routinely punished
For 'behaving like a man'
I've been screamed at for it

Even publicly humiliated for it
But it feels natural to me
To ignore sexist expectations
Where possible. Why should
I be any different?
Be smaller, be quieter
Owe you beautiful
Owe you assimilation
Act abstinent. Only
Be a form of
Entertainment
Be of service
Only devoted
Be sexy
Be purity
Be dumb
Absorb all of this
Sexist abuse
And never speak of it
And if you do, well
You'll be punished
For that too. Expected
Ordained. I know it!
I've experienced it
Over and over again
Haven't we?
It's how the system
Protects itself
It makes an
Example of us

It's why we're all so strung up

The way we disrupt this
Poisonous system is by revaluing
Prioritising, believing, listening to
Loving, loving, loving 'others'
Underrepresented groups
Marginalised people
Each other.

It will help
And protect
Men as well
Of course
That was
Always the plan

It will be amazing
Celebratory, gorgeous
It will be hard, tough
Mind melting
Self actualising
It will be life long
Healing for us all

So, treat me
Like a man please
It's the least you could do.

Black, white, black, black   **M**
Millions of lines of lights   **E**
Streak down, they spin   **T**
They multiply. Teasing us   **A**
Our senses. We can taste   **L**
The rings of suspense
The rising tides. Excitements   **F**
Expectations. Blue, pink   **E**
And purple sights   **S**
Are climbing   **T**
Up. Soaring
We are all wired in   **P**
Please keep provoking us   **O**
Our emotions, our visions   **E**
Musically. I can't contain my   **M**
Buzzing fever. Frenzy
How much I love
Being here or my
Usual roaring anxiety
Though I'm feeling
Much safer here
Much more normal here
The people that I understand
The most are here
My nervousness subsides
It disappears. As I watch these
Epic music creators, designers
Build the waves, the structures

The city scapes
Of sound that surround us
That carefully destroy us
And melt us away
They remake us
We are appreciating
Their expertise
Their invisible
Architecture

As a harmonious unit
They administer the
Medicinal melodies
Tunnelling, spilling
Pointed pieces, notes
Reverberate off the ceiling
They slice through my
Muscles, veins and bones
Answering my questions.
I've been searching
For answers

These alchemists
Soak and bathe us in
Ear-shattering vibrations
You can literally see the
'Will of the Hive Mind'

As we move to the meaty
Dirty, filthy, fixidity. It quenches
My thirsty despicability
Feeding my hunger
For life. For living
It's innocent. It's beautiful
It's the purest music
I have ever heard
Sordid. The chorus' soft
Jagged, jaded drops, jolt
And break me apart
They rip up and
Spit out my
Brainwashed form
My cultural rigidity
It's so nice to be
Cured, for now

Everyone else
Is grinning
Knowing
Supportive
& gunning for
The same things
I can see our
Explicit desires
Waterfalling everywhere
They're on fire! Lit up
By the disgraced music

We share matching aspirations
Everyone I meet is so lovely
Kind, accepting, loving

We understand
Intuitively together
We are lucky to be here
We are lucky to be alive

Losing sh*t
Losing my sh*t
Totally, losing my sh*t
Totally. Like, my things
Like, the VERY
Important things
Like, my keys, cards
Glasses (I can't see nothinggg
F*ck sake. How can
I find stuff like this?!)
Like, objects.
My significant bitsss
Like, my mind. Of course
The crackling panic sets in
The kettle is whistling
As my external, digital
Environment glitches
I catch glimpses
Of pinks and gold
As the surrounding
Space cackles at me
My imagination.
It was just there!
I swear it was
I put it right here!
My imagination?
Am I going crazy?
Not again. Goddamn it...
Sighs. It was just in my hands

L
O
S
I
N
G

M
Y

S
H
*
T

P
O
E
M

I felt it just then!
I thought it was still there
But now it's disappeared
Again. Vanishable. Perishable

I get flashbacks of my
Dad getting *so angry*
When he lost things
The quick mental rewind
Makes my emotions spike
Much more in the present
He got so mad. Jesus.
It felt so scary each time
But now I also feel empathetic
Only of the emotional roller
Coaster he must
Have gone through
Each time. Of the sharply rising
Stress that now - I have to
Actively project manage
Reduce.

Take
Conscious
Breaths
Because if I freak out
And I can't think straight
Then the world won't
Stop flapping
And shaking me

Playing games with me
And my important things
I've misplaced will stay hidden
Sniggering. Hiding and seeking
All of this means
In practice, I'm actually
Incredibly organised
'So disorganised
That I'm organised'
Where I've
Learnt so much
About different systems
Processes
Colour codes
I've labelled
Dozens of boxes
With all my things
Alphabetical. 'Excelled'
As in, I've actually used Excel
To alphabetise them
I'm serious. I know
Hella nerdy! A bit ridiculous really
But be kind to yourself, matey
This complex relationship
With objects is part of your disability
These new organising
Systems come from
All the above distress
So I keep track

Of every thingsss
Of physical bitty reality
All the random bits
And bobs and useful
Essential things.
I regularly sort things out
And it's so full of thought
As I'm proudly giving
Them their rightful place
And I regularly
Give things away to
Reduce the amount
Of items I have. I
Say my goodbyes
My thank yous <3 <3 <3
Less things =
Losing them is less likely
And as a result
Of responding
To all this mess
Nowadays
I'm really great
At organisation
Planning and orderings
Difficulties are
Such blessings
Sometimes. Though they
Don't feel as such at first
They can often become

Our strengths.
Souvenirs.

These learnings
Will always be
Oppositional and
Paradoxical. I'm
Repeating myself again

It's happening again
God. It's so boring.
Labouring
(Do I bore you too?)

I feel like I'm always
Saying and doing
The same things
Repeatedly.
Repeat
Repeat

I'm so sick of myself that
I feel comfortable. My resting mode
Is being trapped. In these familiar
Circular, doings, thinkings
And thoughts

I'm absolutely funked   **M**
Batshit bananas, barmy   **A**
Off the rails. Gone west   **D**
Happily and miserably
Living with my 'craziness'   **P**
With my amped up senses   **R**
                               I
Which can't be anything   **D**
Other than pathologised   **E**
Can they? Can't they?
                               P
Let me play with the stereotypes   **O**
So stuck that I'm performing   **E**
Exactly like my script. Stranded   **M**
Struck. I can't get it off!
It follows me everywhere
No matter what I do

I'm trapped anyway
So I revel in the
Mould that's been
Made for me. We can predict
The future because
All this systemic inequality
Is working like clockwork
Notions of 'madness'
Are intensive tools used
Against the marginalised
They're so effective that

They actually make
You 'go insane'
They force you round
The merry go round
A self fulfilling prophecy
My 'mad' is usually
Pretty all consuming
Pretty all confusing
Compressed reality
Which shakes
And breaks apart.
Can you see it? It's gorgeous
Actually. To watch the
See-through rainbows
Ricochet, zig zag
Shoot across my world
Diagonally. The rectangles
S q u a r e s
Follow the music.
My moods.
I can see the sparks, right there!
My time stretches. I pull it apart
It's sticky as it drips everywhere
As it slows, as it blurs
What comes into my senses
Is the story that meets at the centre
The stress makes it all wax and wane
Makes it spread out, strain, yawn, crack!
The surrounding shapes morph

And change colour.
The objects
Turn to face me.
Why hello there! ^_^
I can feel their bitter energy
Their indifference, mockery
Their comradery
Then my mind recognises
That darkest space
Those vibrant neon lights
And it starts to wrap itself up
In self defence. Fired up. Oh crap
Cracked! Now I can only see a tunnel
That I must mindlessly follow
They tell me that I'm 'crazy'
And they're right. Of course I am
I'm ashen, I've been extinguished
But it doesn't mean I'm wrong
Or that you're always right
Though we will likely always
Get to that same point
Punctuation.
As your words, your world
All this is more recognisable
It's more reassuring, for you
And that's who we are
All prioritising here
We only serve privilege
Remember? And I'm compliant
In my own oppression

I'm your highest paying client
I know I'll be placed somewhere
I can't ever be heard, believed
Or taken seriously
I've shut down but that's okay
Because as I'm mistreated I know that
You're all coming down with me   :)
Sweet, sweet symbiosis

The brain responds
Like this for a reason
To share important lessons
I'm activated. I'm alive
I'm handling it...

These are natural
Protective responses to
That which is beyond computation
Comprehension. I understand now
As the world crashes and burns
Finally, I feel comfortable
Somewhere. As this, now *THIS*
Is something I recognise
The earth is forcing us
Kicking and screaming
To change. I know it in my bones
TBH I've always known that
I was built to survive
This future

One way or the other
We all were. I am at peace
With trying my hardest
Whatever the results
Whatever the
Consequences

I feel so alive
And I recognise that
My psychology
Has simply
Prepared me
For a life on earth
It's trying to do its job
Of self preservation
A conservationist
And I'm really, really
Grateful for that.

'Madness' has
Discarded wisdom
Most of the time
It is there
To increase
The likelihood of
Our survivability

HEAVY METAL   M
Melodic, chunky   E
Trash, industrial, hardcore   T
Alternative, death, death   A
Death metal. A soothing   L
Crash of sounds
Obliterated. A healthy   P
Annihilation. A   O
Deep inhalation   E
                                    M

Patterns flood my vision
They wake up with a start   2
And fiercely shake
As if the energy
Around me is
Buzzing in excitement
The particles are
Intoxicated by
Anticipation

As I climb I wrap myself up in
Consensual and gorgeously
Predictable forms
Of sensory overload
Mathematical
Overwhelm
The numbers
Climb and multiply

The drop is deadly
And I'm dropped
Down, down, down
As the tension
Is released
It's replaced
By a holy
Sense of relief
The drama spirals
Round, round
Round and round
Spinning my endless
Fury and anxiety
Into a peaceful
And clear walkway
Illuminated
I'm siphoning off
Crystal clarity
And I finally
Find my direction.
Fleeting. A rare
Calming method for me
I'm bobbing, nodding
Rocking, stimming
Dancing, singing
Humming
I'm turning
Backwards

No longer stricken
My heart's heavy
Hurting
Stops short
And after a
Hard reverse
I start to ripen

Finally! A gasp of oxygen
This is my 'pillar of hope'
It's juddering, bursting
Bubbling over from
The mechanical
Vibrations

Metal is fulfilling
The greedy needs of my
Trapped treatment
Resistant emotions
Destroying parts
Of my depression
The blockages
The blockades
It's first aid.
I'm a degenerate
And the music's

Dirty corruption
Its cracked forms
Wizz, ping and dart
Across my
Mind and fix
The wires that
Need repairing

U P D A T E   M E

I love all
Good music
But metal
Is at the very top
I've kept it
On a pedestal

It's my musical
S p i r e

Fluffy, floofy, puffy, poofy   C
Soft, cosy, squishy, squashy   O
Comfortable. Fake fur   M
Warm and sensitive   F
Particular. Specialist   Y
Speciality. It will take a lot for me
To change my current happy   P
Nest-like circumstances   O
I appreciate it, I notice that I'm   E
Not uncomfortable, for once!
(God! I'm always uncomfortable   M
Grumpy, grouchy noises here)
I'm surprised. I suddenly realise
I feel so nice and comfy
This is a moment to feel into
To become present through.
Let's do this. Come on!
Whack! Ta da!
I'm finally here!
Present. And it's like
I'm being wrapped up somewhere
Not with wrapping paper but with
A sunny duvet. Luxurious
Like a nice warm bubbly bath
(Without the chemicals)
I'm grateful to
Feel this woolly
Synthetically soft rug
On my feet and toes

For the airy cloud
Feeling I get from
Being in my dressing gown
Or that peaceful feeling I get
From wearing my slippers

I'm quite tactile
Tactfully discerning as a
Way of assessing objects
And products. Such
Judgemental
Examinations

Maybe textures are more
Important to me than I first thought
Not as much as some autistic folk
But I def love what I feel like are
The 'nicest surroundings'

I wrap myself up
In this thick blanket
I am in a cocoon
And I envelop myself
In layers of comfort
So all that's left of me, visibly
Is my dorky, beaming face

The videos, film shots, clips
Cuts. Moving spanning fast images
Recorded, so it's ingrained
Into digital memory
Into my memory too
Though I assume I'm digital

It helps me remember
These beautiful scenes
So I am situated in a nicer place
Forcing myself into better situations

I want to sit and absorb them
I want to sense them so much
To make them all encompassing

I hyper focus into
The most beautiful snippets
When the colours hold and
Complement each other
In a loving healthy relationship
The sounds melt together
And they make me laugh
Stim, or wonder

V
I
D
E
O

E
D
I
T
O
R

P
O
E
M

Static Vision
Squinting
But not telling
In such a clear
But marble
S P A C E.

Seeing
The walls, the floors
Acting, back-grounding

It's raining on my glasses
Dropping black specks
Darting at me!

Opposing
Normal
Vision

P ix
E
L s .

The tiny turning parts
Are usually multicoloured
^_^ yet invisible
Pulsating
breathing!
h e a r t s <3

S
T
A
T
I
C

V
I
S
I
O
N

P
O
E
M

2

97

Sighting tele[visions]
Boxed off as
My
Sensual
Summits

ENERGYSTRANGLED
TurningExcruciationS!
Bruising
In those memories
In those truths

Sometimes when you
Move to a point
The translating veils
Start to vanish
Zipping diamond!
It cutsss
It slits through
In glinting irony

Bleeding.
Pouring...
It's all rushing out!
It's all gushin' out of me

I'm so lucky to have
Been proved wrong
About love and
My lovability

L
O
V
E

Y
O
U
R
S
E
L
F

T
O
D
A
Y

I keep wanting to
Call and message you
But you won't be
There to answer
You are so loved
You are so amazing
I still can't believe it. I can't
I won't. We were just talking
We were just messaging!
But you've gone forever
And I can't accept it at all
I know it now, but I can't bring
Myself to believe it
It is beyond my understanding
You were mid life experience
Mid living. We were mid friendship
It was the very beginning
I hope you know
That you had such an powerful
Impact on so many people
You were part of the
Neurodivergent
Non binary family
How can I ever repay you?
How can I ever repay you now.
I can only hope you are pleased
With your sendoff
I hope we've done you proud
You deserve so much

N
E
L
L
E

P
O
E
M

All your friends are amazing by the way
Just like you were. I wish we had all met
Before. They're so cool, lovely, intelligent
Empathetic. Just like you
The sun shines through the trees
It was like I could feel you in the air
In the comforting natural light
Your friends and I
Held each other, reminiscing
We are holding on through
This inconceivable happening
It makes life unbearable
B r e a k a b l e
The pieces disintegrate in front of me
We don't know how to cope
With missing you and
Your presence
But we have to cope anyway
Some way. This is long, harsh, biting
I'm crying, bursting out sadness
And anger. And love, appreciation
Remembering, laughing
Celebrating your brilliant life
We were all there to celebrate you
And to mourn you. Old friends
Best friends, new connections
Familiar, comforting strangers
Metal heads, mental health
Adventurers, navigators
So many folks from the

Autistic queer
Trans community
Working out how to
Support each other
I'm filled with disbelief
Cathartic and natural insanity
But for once and with your friends
At the same time
I feel comfortable somewhere
Right here. I can grieve in peace
These are people I can relate to
Remember with
I don't want to
Accept that
Now all things
Have to be done without you
Now. I don't know how
To handle these feelings
And I'm so grateful, sad
It feels more than
Understandable
That others seem
To feel the same
It's the only thing
That makes any sense
All the best words are
Not enough to describe you
Or how much you meant to us
This world is so bitter and sweet

I can't deal with it. I won't
What can I do with myself?
I have to exist here and
Manage these
Circumstances.
This new and emptier
Reality settles in

We will always
Miss you

We will always
Celebrate you

You unforgettable
Rock
Star

So endlessly stressed right now
So, my body and mind hurt
I feel like a forest fire
And I'm brought back down to my body
A rarity. I'm live, on air. I'm published
There are times the pain reduces
Increases, it moves.
Like it's dancing within me
In line with my physical movements
And my physical commitments
Let's hope I can start again
In a wiser, aged place
In a better place
I can't 'do much' right now
On occasions
And it feels horrible
Like how, when
Waking up was painful
It makes sense people are too busy
For all the levels of my needs
They are my own responsibility
But we all suffer in life
And we take care of each other
We look out for one another
In community. It's basic
It's tag and I've timed out
Gamed over
FATALITIED. K'O'D
In any case, some time alone
Works well for me as I need

S
T
R
E
S
S
E
D

O
P
P
R
E
S
S
E
D

P
O
E
M

To do surgery on myself
In my emergency room
I need to feel my truth
To repair all the damage
I zoom in and expertly fix
What's broken. It's an enormous effort
But I take care of myself perfectly
Expertly. Now I'm within my means
My capacity. And some folks
Check in to see how things
Are going. We have some
Fun laughing snippets. Small
Meaningful moments that act as
The basis of living
We talk at length and I
Finally feel seen
We take shifts so that
Whilst someone is suffering
We make sure they
Are taken care of
We keep watch
With the widest binoculars
The largest weapons
And defensive technologies
My oozing, colourful, moody pain
That shocks me like electricity
Starts to changes tack
And soften

Like, it's changed its mind
The gift of friendship
(I know I'm so corny)
Is eating up my 'crazy'

The support
Lights me up differently
As the new information
Seeps in. I turn over
Repositioning

That's better!
Now I feel much
More comfortable
Like life's painkillers
Are working away
And even my
Physical pain
Gets better
Still moving and making sounds
So I can integrate into the music
So I become a part of it
Melting into something else

Love and music
Heals my world
They make life
Indescribably
Good and
Meaning full

All my hidden elements
Have transpired
They have been
Revealed to you
I am exposed. And, you ask
Why do I go by 'they' 'them'
Ideally? Because I am not a woman
And I have never felt like one
I don't belong to that category
I identify somewhat with women
Because I am seen as one
And socialised as such
I experience the same
Usual sexism as women
The same gendered
Expectations. Because of
Other peoples assumptions
I can see the insights, some of the views
Some of the perspectives from women's
Experiences. But I have
Always felt like 'more'
Then the binding references
This world gives me
Not superior, not better
But beyond binaries
To me, I make the most sense
To me. Of course. When people
Call me 'she' they
Mean no harm

T
H
E
Y
/
T
H
E
M

P
O
E
M

And I don't always
Judge them for it
But it feels wrong
Uncomfortable
It actually hurts
Each time. Yet I know that
It will always happen. I know that
They don't mean anything
By it 99.9% of the time
Also it changes, like at work
I am flexible, with people I don't know
Even though it still hurts
It's more permissible
It still hurts less than being
A 'they' all the time
In this culture. And yknow
I'd rather be accommodating
I know it's not great but
That's my brand of brainwashing
It's what feels natural to me
Most comfortable. I remember
When our spiritual
Teacher called me
'An insult to women'
So-called spiritual teachers
Can be so full of sh*t, you know
But I didn't realise that at the time
That comment really hit me. But in some
Ways I guess I am an insult

To modern notions of this category
To 'woman'. To how the modern
World works. I'm offensive to abusive
Norms. Shocking. Shaking.

Let's keep making
Excessive privileges
Feel self conscious
Let's threaten the status quo
I am in the middle of it
Of this bickering hetero
Normative 'oppositional'
Couple, I'm in the
Inbetweenness

Dropping through
The cracks
I'm comfortable
As I endlessly fall
Not to be arrogant
But conceptually
My existing challenges
These theoretical
Understandings
Assumptions. Proudly
I'm meant to insult
I'm meant to offend
I'm meant to break a part
The ways we categorise the world

Nature has its own moods
And different areas have
Their own themes
Their own types of music

Can you hear it?
We're so lucky to have
Our own earth-grown festival

Yesterday we
Explored
Spaced out
Pale yellow
Green and white
Parts of the forest
It looked like such
Thoughtful artistry
And I loved the
Crunching
Beneath my feet

I had to *really*
Focus to be there
Because getting
Into my body
Is a lot of active
Labour
And I did it
With the help
Of the forest
Thank you forest!

N
A
T
U
R
E

P
O
E
M

We played Battleships
By the lake on
The picnic bench
With a flask of tea

I was greedily, eagerly
Collecting my winnings
And positive experiences

The sun setting
Looked like
A red and yellow
Autumn sound
And I could see
Such incredible
Plump clouds
As well as the trees'
Reflection in the lake
Just. Wow

I wonder what else I can do
To help protect nature...

When I'm being blocked
Where I'm not being fulfilled
Or allowed to push myself
To my potential
When my path is being ignored
My accuracy, knowledge
And criticality being undermined
Ridiculed. As it is wrongly
Seen as a threat
And not an asset

I feel like a wasted
Form of potency
Squandered life-force
What a needless waste
But it's not useless to me
As this urgency is set in place
Pushing me on the right path

But it feels ugly
Like I am tied up
In unbending reality
Working tirelessly
Exhaustively towards
Fleeting opportunities
Let's carry on, on
The permanent
Task of finding
Where one belongs

WORKPLACE

BULLYING

POEM

2

Grief tears   G
Everything apart   R
The world has gotten   I
So much darker   E
And we become   F
Naturally alone

                                         P
Grief pulls   O
People together   E
It can help us   M
Appreciate life
Because it elicits Love
Because we don't know   2
When life will stop

It can help refine
The time we have left
And maybe that's the reason
Why everything comes to an end

So whilst we are here
Let's compassion, let's joy.
Let's love. Let's hold on
And bloom, my
Amazings.
Hold on

My family
Is in a state
Of permanent
Collapse.
World ending.
These are my roots
My sense of safety
My sense of Self

S
U
R
V
I
V
I
N
G

D
.
A
.

P
O
E
M

2

Be direct with me
As I'll always think
You're being literal
That you mean
What you say
I know – how unusual!
To expect sincerity
But that's my software
That's how I've been
Programmed
And unlike my society
I don't experience
It as a problem
I think it's beautiful

D
I
R
E
C
T
N
E
S
S

P
O
E
M

Chronic pain   C
Impacts more people   H
Than I thought   R
Invisibly targeting   O
Their energy   N
Their mood   I
For me it comes suddenly   C
! Feels unending
All consuming   P
Eating up   A
My consciousness   I
Delicious misery   N
Num num nam. But stops
Then changes unexpectedly   P
Great. Something else to manage   O
And my cup feels full   E
Not in a 'good'   M
Oppressively positive way
My 'Spoons' are less so
It limits my left over energy
And things that seem
Simple for others
Can be more
Complex and
Difficult for me
It takes even MY effort
To help people 'see'
If only they empathised
Naturally

I make sure my time
My connections count
To try and only focus on
Nutritious and
Fun moments
They become
Uniquely potent
Meaningful
Healthy relationships
Are a necessity and
I have no energy
To waste on bullsh*t
And toxicity

I feel strong for coping
Strong for enduring
For laughing
(My dark humour
Saves me)
For still being loving
Through all the meanness
Life can deal out

Don't worry
You're also allowed
To be grumpy! Just like you
I've managed too many
Hidden, unexpected

Challenges. I know I can
Deal with almost anything
It's quite the confidence

I'm 'strong in the real way'
Go me! Growing up around disability
Despite my culture and treatment
Medically, I know innately
That I am worthy, important
And have great value
Just like you

When I fight back
I am blamed. Hell.
I am burned.

Such
Double
Standardsss.
& I am cracking.
sizzzzling. Damn
Our raging anger
Kills all our
Favourite things including
All our favourite plants
So it's not great...
Even if the feelings
Are justifiable
They're also
Uncontrollable

Our light lives on
Always deep down
In the depths
In the unknown

Perfect. I am constantly
Demonised after all
Of course
It is only natural
To crumble.
Into particles

S
C
O
R
P
I
O
N
I
C

G
E
N
E
R
A
T
I
O
N

P
O
E
M

We seep into all realities.
We expand everywhere.

I can see
That frightens you
And I just pity you.

Keep remembering
That killing me
Doesn't work

I'll
Always
Come back

I'm a loser   L
What's the problem?   O
I lost the game   S
A long time ago   E
It wasn't made   R
For the likes of me
Wait, wait, wait, wait   P
What are we fighting over again?   O
To be right? For the male gaze?   E
Okay, um. If it was   M
Something worthwhile
Wouldn't we all be first together?
My people were
Always the aliens
The sullied, the jaded
The real. We're live
I know I'm a loser
The last to laugh
As I slowly understand
The rules. This Kingdom.
That we've been set up
We lost! I'm the butt
Of sh*t jokes
Asking for it' really.
I mean, look at me!
Made for it.
Born for it. 'Crazy'
We are society's trash

An optimum place
To stub out the
World's insecurities

Breathe it all in!
The luscious
Addictive smoke
The potent chemicals
They make me mutate

My beautiful
Failing, falling
Flat on my face
Pleased to say
I'm losing
The popularity
Contest in style
They always put
Me in last place
Thank Christ!
Mistakes. Mishaps
Miss shape, Misfitted
I make sure to
Regularly
Celebrate my life
That's retrograding
It makes for
The best stories

The fastest
Types of learning
Forms of evolving
It's why instead
You're so stuck
In one place
But that's not
My problem.
Your karma

That's my in joke.
My opportunistic failures
I find it so amusing
This queer story
I'm the comic
Of my own life and
It's a hell of a lot of fun

So. Do you really want to win
The earth's sickest game?
Are you sure about that?
I'd rather be laughing last
I'd rather be a loser

Faerytales
Thirsty for knowledge
For nourishment. Go on!
Enrich me curiosity!
Thoughts blurt, tumble
Crash. Burst! Flood
They collapse out of us.
Some walk through us
Smugly. So smart and neatly
I'm just so amused
Giggling, coughing as
We stir our concoctions
Let's make mind alchemy!
I mean. Humans just intrigue me.
Don't you think? I mean.
Truly. What the hell
My mind ticks over
After our conversation
After our facial expressions
They stay with me for decades
All those times
All those eyes made contact
Hello! Sharp, spiked
Splintered disdain or
Warm, loving, friendly times
I'm constantly exposed to
Different windows to the soul

F
A
E
R
Y
T
A
L
E
S

P
O
E
M

Yelping. Shining through
Clasping. I want to cover my
Eyes and ears as
The particles start up
Illuminating compatibility
Illuminating incompatibility
All in small moments
All in time that slows
That intensifies

I burst
In speech
Through
Movement
And colours.
Only in blues, pinks
And violets

And together in awkward
Human bodies and existence
We use movement to
Manage these complexities
To constantly flow
Like life blood
We build and twist and turn
And focusing on the rhythms
We make. We are booming, happy
Thumping; connected

Communitied.
Communicated.
This is life altering
Alternating.
We are always raising
Disseminating
Energy. This is
Our most
Natural state.

You can make
That source
Appear, familiar
I mean, what do
You feel like
Now?

Certainly some
/one/where else
No longer categorical.
It's a gift, I think.
One we all have

Paradox as
Profound irony.
We are watching
Closely. Interested
In all these
Graphic stories

We are all *so* interested in
How love, pain, humour
Suffering and
Compassion
Violently
Transform
Everything.

Can you see it?
I bet you see it now
That all I talk about is
Contradiction. A most
Natural thing
Yawn, stretch
Time to rest soon
Truth is, what I
Really want to -
What I've been trying
To say is that
It's these
Simple
Oppressive
Oppositional
Categories
They are
What is ultimately
I n c o m p r e h e n s i b l e
They are unforgivable.

The sea is so beautiful   **B**
Here on my own   **E**
I lie on the stones   **E**
Resting and listening   **T**
Humming to my true music   **L**
I curl up to rest and   **E**
As I'm watching the waves
I ground myself in nature   **P**
I walk around singing   **O**
And humming   **E**
I'm a happy dork and   **M**
I watch past memories
Flicker through my mind
I'm enjoying the familiar path
I plod along to. That I belong to
I find some more nature
And settle on the grass
Opposite all the flowers
I watch them move in the wind
With my face in the greenness
I'm enjoying it so much!
A while later a beetle walks by
They symbolise strength
In unlikely places. & I really hope
That's a good sign for me

Thank you so much for reading this work. I really appreciate it.

Poetry is made for sharing, so if you know anyone who might relate to and feel comforted by my poetry, please share it with them.

Thank you to everyone who has sent such loving and affirming feedback about my poems. You have made such a difference to my confidence and made this book possible!

Thanks to my pal Karen for all of your help with this book and your fantastic encouragement and friendship. You are a legend.

You can keep in touch by following me on YouTube (Nadia The Poet) or TikTok (Nadia.The.Poet). If you enjoyed the book, please leave a review on Amazon. Thank you very much for reading!

– Nadia Violette

Nadia is a proud autistic, non binary, queer, S.A./ D.A. survivor and chronically ill person. They've worked and volunteered in many fields including renewable energy, climate activism, mental and sexual health, disability, diversity and communications work.

They have an MA in Gender, Policy and Inequality from the London School of Economics, and they create spoken word, comedy and educational videos on TikTok and YouTube.

The first time they wrote a poem, they were writing down exactly what their mental health spiral felt like on a train journey. Their suffering had suddenly become art that others related to which helped Nadia feel much better and less alone. For the first time, they felt understood by others. The rest is history.

The kind encouragement they received from their loved ones, and from people who strongly related to their work, kept them writing. This collection spans over the last 13 years of their life. They hope these poems help you feel affirmed, seen, informed, loved, joyous and less alone, as well as inspired to make your own poetry.

May these playful, painful, hopeful words resonate with you and support you, as they have done for Nadia.

www.tiktok.com/@Nadia.The.Poet
www.youtube.com/@NadiaThePoet

Printed in Great Britain
by Amazon

24132966R00076